"I love my gratitude journal
I have written daily gratitudes on and off for many years, and EVERY day since September 2015. Your journal has been a fantastic tool for recording. The achievements page is awesome, on those days when you think you haven't achieved much, this prompts you to acknowledge all the little things that you do get done!! I have just finished my first journal and have my second ready to go."

Kathryn Hammond
Owner, Action Organising

"I love my journal and am so grateful for it.
I get inspired each and every time I write in it.
I also find a lot of communication comes from my guides with it. My daily gratitude practice has lead me to this wonderful space of high vibration, flow, and alignment and I love it.
Thank you for this beautiful creation <3"

Shaz Cini
Owner, Shaz Cini

"I've been lucky enough to be gifted a copy of Kylie's book, *Today, I am Grateful*. Daily Affirmations is not something I've done before but thought I would step outside my comfort zone and give it a go. I've really been enjoying completing this each evening and taking pleasure in life's simple pleasures. I strongly encourage you to get your own copy and make it apart of your daily routine."

Emma Warren
Owner, Emma Warren –
Independent Norwex Consultant

"The gratitude journal from Kylie King – The Phoenix Within has been one of the most helpful tools for me in my journey to being free to be myself!

It is absolutely beautifully set out, has really helpful prompts when sometimes it can feel hard to know what to be grateful for.

I actually appreciate the no date because I didn't feel guilty if I missed a day or too and could pick off from where I left but could add the date if I wanted to specifically remember something from that day!

The thing I loved most about this journal was the area to celebrate wins/achievements to reflect on the positive things and to remember they didn't have to be life changing but life giving – things that reminded me of my strengths or the things that reminded I got through the day or the simple reminders my kids would give me like "I love you" or "You are the best mummy" or "Thank you".

It has really helped me in my mindset and it really helps me to put life into perspective and bring a smile to my face. I often so mind in the morning for the day before as it helps me to start the day feeling positive.

I seriously want a never ending supply of journals even a 365 day one to get me through the year 😊☺.

Thank you Kylie! I may have to purchase a few for Christmas gifts too. I love it, the heart behind it and supporting such a wonderful small business. ♥"

Naomi Pike
Owner, Naomi Pike –
Independent Norwex Consultant

Today, I am Grateful

90 days of
gratitude, achievement
and feedback

Today, I am Grateful

90 days of
gratitude, achievement
and feedback

Kylie King

2020

Copyright © 2020 by Kylie King – The Phoenix Within

All rights reserved. This book or any portion thereof may not be reproduced or used in any manner whatsoever without the express written permission of the publisher except for the use of brief quotations in a book review or scholarly journal.

ISBN: 978-0-6452306-1-1
First Printing: 2020

The Phoenix Within
Faulconbridge, NSW 2776

www.thephoenixwithin.com.au

Cover and Internal pages designed by Domenika Fairy
Email: dfairy@internode.on.net

Australian trade bookstores and wholesalers:
Please contact The Phoenix Within
Tel: 0415 561 828 or email kylie@thephoenixwithin.com.au

Dedication

Hello there, you amazing person!
I dedicate this book to you.

Congratulations on taking the first steps
to starting your new lifestyle.

By practicing gratitude, documenting your achievements
and taking note of positive feedback you receive,
not only will your mindset change but also your outlook.

You've got this!!

Introduction

A few people have asked me how this journal came to be. I am a night owl so was up late working on content for my clients and finally at 3am I made the decision it was time to head to bed, as soon as my head hit the pillow – the idea for the journal came to be.

When I started my journey into personal development, I wanted to ensure I had a sturdy foundation to build everything on to. What I mean by this is I wanted my foundation to be strong, made of concrete and steel not just stuck together with chewing gum and masking tape.

My first goals were to look at how I could establish this foundation for my mindset, so I could keep a positive mindset.

I realised that a lot of my clients are also at the beginning of their self-development journey and may not have a solid foundation to build on.

Having a positive mindset and starting and ending your day in the right mindset is a great solid foundation for your personal development journey.

A great way to do this is to practice daily gratitude, take note of your achievements and record any positive feedback you receive.

When I start working with a client, the first thing I ask is do they practice daily gratitude? A lot of them haven't. Then I noticed they tend to overthink the way to do it and would ask questions like, "Do I need a specific journal?" "How do I do this?"

To make this process easy – this journal was born. Here is a great brick to add to your foundation for your personal development journey.

Thank you to everyone who has purchased a copy and supported this 3am idea, I honestly did not think that I would sell a single copy and now I am honoured to say this journal has copies not only around Australia but also in Spain, Romania, Canada and the UK.

I am grateful every day for the amazing work this journal has achieved so far.

What is Gratitude?

Gratitude is an emotion that relates to our ability to feel and express appreciation and thankfulness.

Gratitude is that warm feeling you get when you remember that person who paid for your petrol at the service station when your card was declined or when you're a brand new mum and your neighbor turns up at your door with a home cooked meal so you don't have to worry about how you will feed yourself and juggle a newborn.

It has also been recognized that gratitude is associated with mental health. In 2007, Robert Emmons began researching gratitude. He found that expressing your gratitude improves not only your mental health but also your physical and relational wellbeing. He concluded that being grateful also impacted the overall experience of happiness and these effects tended to be long-lasting.

The most common method to express your gratitude is by recording your experiences in a "Gratitude Journal." In this journal, we have included 5 daily bullet points to start your new habit.
At first it may feel hard to fill in all 5 but like any new skill, practice makes perfect.

Any experience that makes you feel thankful or appreciative should be included in this gratitude journal. Examples include: receiving a hug from your son or daughter, a great catch up with a friend, helping someone solve a problem or a good cup of tea.

Why is Practicing Gratitude Important?

There are so many benefits to practicing gratitude and the practice is as easy as opening up a journal such as this one and writing down instances, experiences or things from the day that you are truly grateful for.

Benefits of practicing gratitude include:

- Gratitude improves your physical health
- Gratitude enhances empathy and reduces aggression
- Grateful people sleep better
- Gratitude improves self-esteem
- Grateful people have stronger immune systems.
- Grateful people have heightened spirituality which means they have the ability to see something bigger than themselves.
- Gratitude improves your optimism and happiness.

Gratitude doesn't need to be reserved only for big occasions - like the birth of a baby, a promotion or a pay rise. You can be thankful for something as simple as a piece of yummy cake.

Gratitude Prompts

Feeling stuck?
Unsure of what to write down?
Here are some prompts to get the grateful vibes flowing.

- Self-Love
- Health
- Work
- Partner/Spouse
- Pets
- Family
- Food
- Home
- Hobby
- Travel
- Technology
- Body
- Senses
- Accomplishments
- Friends
- Weather
- Books
- Before Bed
- When You Wake Up
- Music

- Challenges
- Failures
- Quiet
- Noise
- Feelings
- Mind
- Opportunities
- Nature
- Favourite Things
- City You Live In
- Heritage
- Past
- Job/Occupation
- Favourite Memory
- Lessons Learned This Year
- Someone Who Inspires You
- Knowledge
- Love
- Season
- Colour

- Kindness
- Food
- Talent
- Something that keeps me safe
- Something I've done to help others
- Possession
- Traditions
- Struggles
- Time
- Lessons
- Laughter
- Finances
- Experiences
- Values
- Abilities
- Adventures
- Routines
- Comfort
- A Gift
- Something You Do Everyday
- Smell
- Smile
- Spontaneity
- Someone Who's Older
- Transportation
- Myself
- Passion
- Purpose
- Letting Go
- Sunshine
- Words
- Sunrise
- Sunset
- Morning
- Afternoon
- Evening

Document those achievements!

It is so easy to fall into that thought process of concentrating on everything you haven't accomplished, and it can be demotivating.

Let's face it there is always a never-ending to-do list, constant distractions such as housework, etc. I used to find myself regularly going to bed feeling like I hadn't achieved anything and that I was like a car stuck in the mud with my wheels rolling and going nowhere. These thoughts would keep me up at night.

To silence these thoughts, I started to write down 3 things that I accomplished each day. Big or small it didn't matter as they are all achievements, for example:
I managed to last a day with no kid vomit on my shirt – TICK.
Reached the bottom of my laundry hamper – TICK.
Finished off a PowerPoint for an upcoming presentation – TICK.

It is important to focus on what YOU did do, rather than what you didn't.

By writing down 3 achievements from my day, I was able to go to bed feeling accomplished and relaxed.

Include what you're proud of, what you loved doing, a challenge you faced or a problem you solved. Note the actions you took and the outcomes.

Don't include every single thing you did during the day, or busy work. Being busy is not an achievement. It may feel great in the moment but be honest, do you want to remember when you spent 2 hours billing clients or 4 hours scheduling social media posts.

Remember, every small achievement is a triumph!

Compliments vs Complaints - Feedback

How many times have you received a compliment from someone and simply smiled and said, "Thanks" and continued on with your day?

How often do you think about that compliment afterwards?

Now, let's compare it to its opposite – the complaint. How do you deal with it?

Usually, we receive a complaint, or a criticism and we think about it, we dwell on it. Then we put time into how we can work on it and overcome this.

If you're similar to me, you may receive a dozen compliments a day and then when one criticism is given, all of those compliments are thrown out the window as I turn my focus onto that one complaint. What's up with that?

Now at the end of the day when you are ready to let your head hit the pillow, I want you to take a moment to think back to the compliments you received today and jot them down.

By completing this process alone, it helps you to finish the day on a strong note. So, write down those compliments and refer back to them whenever you are feeling low or need a reminder of how truly amazing you are!

Why 90 days?

Did you know?

It takes 21 days to build or break a habit and 90 days to create a lifestyle.

The 21/90 rule is a great tool to use to create a new habit.

New habits can be hard to put into place even if you have the best intentions and it's a good habit. This is also the same when you are trying to break a habit.

The 21/90 rule simply states as written above.
Commit to a goal for a straight 21 days and it will become a habit. If you are consistent with this goal for 90 days, it will become a part of your daily routine and thus a part of your lifestyle.

This journal is for 90 days.

This is to ensure that we turn this routine not only into a habit but also, so it becomes a part of your daily routine and your lifestyle.

Now is the time to take 10 minutes at the start of the day or 10 minutes before you go to sleep to practice gratitude, record your achievements and taking note of the compliments you received today.

I look forward to hearing how your 90 days went once you complete this journal.

Today, I am Grateful

Gratitude

What are you thankful for today?

-
-
-
-
-

Quote

"Gratitude turns what we have into enough."
Anonymous

Achievements

What did you achieve today?
Big or small – they're all important.

- _____
  _____
  _____

- _____
  _____
  _____

- _____
  _____
  _____

Feedback

Share one compliment you received today.

_____
_____
_____
_____

Awesome work!!

Gratitude

What are you thankful for today?

- _____

- _____

- _____

- _____

Quote

"Feeling gratitude and not expressing it is like wrapping a present and not giving it."
William Arthur Ward

Achievements

What did you achieve today?
Big or small – they're all important.

Feedback

Share one compliment you received today.

Awesome work!!

Gratitude

What are you thankful for today?

-
-
-
-

Affirmation

I am grateful for excellent health, prosperity and true love.

Achievements

What did you achieve today?
Big or small – they're all important.

-
-
-

Feedback

Share one compliment you received today.

Awesome work!!

Gratitude

What are you thankful for today?

- _____

- _____

- _____

- _____

- _____

Affirmation

I am blessed.

Achievements

What did you achieve today?
Big or small – they're all important.

-
-
-

Feedback

Share one compliment you received today.

Awesome work!!

Gratitude

What are you thankful for today?

-
-
-
-
-

Quote

"This a wonderful day. I've never seen this one before."
Maya Angelou.

Achievements

What did you achieve today?
Big or small – they're all important.

_____

_____

_____

_____

_____

_____

_____

_____

_____

Feedback

Share one compliment you received today.

_____

_____

_____

_____

Awesome work!!

Gratitude

What are you thankful for today?

-
-
-
-
-

Quote

"Gratitude is not only the greatest of virtues, but the parent of all the others."
Cicero

Achievements

What did you achieve today?
Big or small – they're all important.

-
-
-

Feedback

Share one compliment you received today.

Awesome work!!

Gratitude

What are you thankful for today?

-
-
-
-

Quote

"Gratitude is riches.
Complaint is poverty."
Doris Day

Achievements

What did you achieve today?
Big or small – they're all important.

Feedback

Share one compliment you received today.

Awesome work!!

Gratitude

What are you thankful for today?

-
-
-
-
-

Affirmation

I am so grateful for supportive friends and a loving family.

Achievements

What did you achieve today?
Big or small – they're all important.

-
-
-

Feedback

Share one compliment you received today.

Awesome work!!

Gratitude

What are you thankful for today?

-
-
-
-
-

Affirmation

All challenges are an opportunity for growth and I am thankful for the chance to evolve.

Achievements

What did you achieve today?
Big or small – they're all important.

Feedback

Share one compliment you received today.

Awesome work!!

Gratitude

What are you thankful for today?

-
-
-
-
-

Quote

"Some people grumble that roses have thorns; I am grateful that thorns have roses."
Alphonse Karr

Achievements

What did you achieve today?
Big or small – they're all important.

-
-
-

Feedback

Share one compliment you received today.

Awesome work!!

Gratitude

What are you thankful for today?

- _____
  _____
  _____

- _____
  _____
  _____
  _____

- _____
  _____
  _____
  _____

- _____
  _____
  _____

- _____
  _____

Quote

"Gratitude is the healthiest of all human emotions. The more you express gratitude for what you have, the more likely you will have even more to express gratitude for."
Zig Ziglar

Achievements

What did you achieve today?
Big or small – they're all important.

- _____
- _____
- _____

Feedback

Share one compliment you received today.

_____

Awesome work!!

Gratitude

What are you thankful for today?

-
-
-
-
-

Affirmation

I am grateful for excellent health, prosperity and true love.

Achievements

What did you achieve today?
Big or small – they're all important.

-
-
-

Feedback

Share one compliment you received today.

Awesome work!!

Gratitude

What are you thankful for today?

- _____
  _____
  _____
  _____

- _____
  _____
  _____
  _____

- _____
  _____
  _____
  _____

- _____
  _____
  _____
  _____

- _____
  _____
  _____

Affirmation

In truth, my gratitude is an absolute magnet for the manifestation of all that I want.

Achievements

What did you achieve today?
Big or small – they're all important.

-
-
-

Feedback

Share one compliment you received today.

Awesome work!!

Gratitude

What are you thankful for today?

-
-
-
-
-

Quote

"Thankfulness is the beginning of gratitude. Gratitude is the completion of thankfulness. Thankfulness may consist merely of words. Gratitude is shown in acts."
Henri Frederic Amiel

Achievements

What did you achieve today?
Big or small – they're all important.

-
-
-

Feedback

Share one compliment you received today.

Awesome work!!

Gratitude

What are you thankful for today?

-
-
-
-
-

Quote

"What separates privilege from entitlement is gratitude."
Brene Brown

Achievements

What did you achieve today?
Big or small – they're all important.

-
-
-

Feedback

Share one compliment you received today.

Awesome work!!

Gratitude

What are you thankful for today?

-
-
-
-
-

I feel gratitude for everything.

Achievements

What did you achieve today?
Big or small – they're all important.

-
-
-

Feedback

Share one compliment you received today.

Awesome work!!

Gratitude

What are you thankful for today?

-
-
-
-
-

Affirmation

I am learning to be grateful for what I have while being excited for what has yet to come.

Achievements

What did you achieve today?
Big or small – they're all important.

-
-
-

Feedback

Share one compliment you received today.

Awesome work!!

Gratitude

What are you thankful for today?

-
-
-
-
-

Quote

"When I started counting my blessings, my whole life turned around."
Willie Nelson

Achievements

What did you achieve today?
Big or small – they're all important.

-
-
-

Feedback

Share one compliment you received today.

Awesome work!!

Gratitude

What are you thankful for today?

-
-
-
-
-

Quote

"Gratitude is a currency that we can mint for ourselves and spend without fear of bankruptcy."
Fred De Witt Van Amburgh

Achievements

What did you achieve today?
Big or small – they're all important.

Feedback

Share one compliment you received today.

Awesome work!!

Gratitude

What are you thankful for today?

-
-
-
-
-

Affirmation

I am grateful now, and that is keeping the door open for more blessings.

Achievements

What did you achieve today?
Big or small – they're all important.

-
-
-

Feedback

Share one compliment you received today.

Awesome work!!

Gratitude

What are you thankful for today?

- _____
  _____
  _____

- _____
  _____
  _____

- _____
  _____
  _____

- _____
  _____
  _____

Affirmation

Whatever has happened, and whatever does happen, I'm certain that I can be grateful again.

Achievements

What did you achieve today?
Big or small – they're all important.

Feedback

Share one compliment you received today.

Awesome work!!

Gratitude

What are you thankful for today?

-
-
-
-
-

Quote

"Piglet noticed that even though he had a Very Small Heart, it could hold a rather large amount of Gratitude."
A.A. Milne

Achievements

What did you achieve today?
Big or small – they're all important.

-
-
-

Feedback

Share one compliment you received today.

Awesome work!!

Gratitude

What are you thankful for today?

-
-
-
-
-

Quote

"Forget yesterday it has already forgotten you. Don't sweat tomorrow you haven't even met. Instead, open your eyes and your heart to a truly precious gift today."
Steve Maraboli

Achievements

What did you achieve today?
Big or small – they're all important.

-
-
-

Feedback

Share one compliment you received today.

Awesome work!!

Gratitude

What are you thankful for today?

-
-
-
-

Affirmation

The feeling of gratefulness expands my perspective and opens me up to new ways of living happily in this world; it's as if the whole universe is in my heart.

Achievements

What did you achieve today?
Big or small – they're all important.

- _____

- _____

- _____

Feedback

Share one compliment you received today.

_____

Awesome work!!

Gratitude

What are you thankful for today?

- _____

- _____

- _____

- _____

- _____

Affirmation

I give thanks for the helpful spirits and ancestors that guide me in this life journey.

Achievements

What did you achieve today?
Big or small – they're all important.

- _____
- _____
- _____

Feedback

Share one compliment you received today.

_____

Awesome work!!

Gratitude

What are you thankful for today?

-
-
-
-
-

Quote

"The longer you linger in gratitude, the more you draw your new life to you. For gratitude is the ultimate state of receivership."
Dr. Joe Dispenza

Achievements

What did you achieve today?
Big or small – they're all important.

-
-
-

Feedback

Share one compliment you received today.

Awesome work!!

Gratitude

What are you thankful for today?

- _____

- _____

- _____

- _____

- _____

Proverb

"'Enough' is a feast."
Buddhist proverb

Achievements

What did you achieve today?
Big or small – they're all important.

Feedback

Share one compliment you received today.

Awesome work!!

Gratitude

What are you thankful for today?

-
-
-
-
-

Quote

"Gratitude turns what we have into enough."
Anonymous.

Achievements

What did you achieve today?
Big or small – they're all important.

- _____

- _____

- _____

Feedback

Share one compliment you received today.

_____

Awesome work!!

Gratitude

What are you thankful for today?

-
-
-
-

Quote

"Feeling gratitude and not expressing it is like wrapping a present and not giving it."
William Arthur Ward

Achievements

What did you achieve today?
Big or small – they're all important.

-
-
-

Feedback

Share one compliment you received today.

Awesome work!!

CONGRATULATIONS
ON REACHING DAY
30!!

Gratitude

Review your last 30 days of Gratitude and record your Top 5 here.

- _____

- _____

- _____

- _____

- _____

Achievements

Review your last 30 days of Achievements and record your Top 3.

- _____
  _____
  _____

- _____
  _____
  _____
  _____

- _____
  _____
  _____

Feedback

Review your last 30 days of Feedback and record your Top 2.

_____
_____
_____

YOU HAVE NOW MADE THIS A HABIT!!

Gratitude

What are you thankful for today?

-
-
-
-
-

Affirmation

I am grateful for excellent health, prosperity and true love.

Achievements

What did you achieve today?
Big or small – they're all important.

-

-

-

Feedback

Share one compliment you received today.

Awesome work!!

Gratitude

What are you thankful for today?

-
-
-
-

Affirmation

I am blessed.

Achievements

What did you achieve today?
Big or small – they're all important.

-
-
-

Feedback

Share one compliment you received today.

Awesome work!!

Gratitude

What are you thankful for today?

-
-
-
-
-

Quote

"This a wonderful day. I've never seen this one before."
Maya Angelou.

Achievements

What did you achieve today?
Big or small – they're all important.

Feedback

Share one compliment you received today.

Awesome work!!

Gratitude

What are you thankful for today?

-
-
-
-
-

Quote

"Gratitude is not only the greatest of virtues, but the parent of all the others."
Cicero

Achievements

What did you achieve today?
Big or small – they're all important.

Feedback

Share one compliment you received today.

Awesome work!!

Gratitude

What are you thankful for today?

-
-
-
-
-

Quote

"Gratitude is riches. Complaint is poverty."
Doris Day

Achievements

What did you achieve today?
Big or small – they're all important.

-
-
-

Feedback

Share one compliment you received today.

Awesome work!!

Gratitude

What are you thankful for today?

-
-
-
-

Affirmation

I am so grateful for supportive friends and a loving family.

Achievements

What did you achieve today?
Big or small – they're all important.

Feedback

Share one compliment you received today.

Awesome work!!

Gratitude

What are you thankful for today?

-
-
-
-

Affirmation

All challenges are an opportunity for growth and I am thankful for the chance to evolve.

Achievements

What did you achieve today?
Big or small – they're all important.

-
-
-

Feedback

Share one compliment you received today.

Awesome work!!

Gratitude

What are you thankful for today?

-
-
-
-

Quote

"Some people grumble that roses have thorns; I am grateful that thorns have roses."
Alphonse Karr

Achievements

What did you achieve today?
Big or small – they're all important.

-
-
-

Feedback

Share one compliment you received today.

Awesome work!!

Gratitude

What are you thankful for today?

-
-
-
-
-

Quote

"Gratitude is the healthiest of all human emotions. The more you express gratitude for what you have, the more likely you will have even more to express gratitude for."
Zig Ziglar

Achievements

What did you achieve today?
Big or small – they're all important.

-
-
-

Feedback

Share one compliment you received today.

Awesome work!!

Gratitude

What are you thankful for today?

-
-
-
-
-

Affirmation

I am grateful for excellent health, prosperity and true love.

Achievements

What did you achieve today?
Big or small – they're all important.

- _____
  _____
  _____

- _____
  _____
  _____

- _____
  _____
  _____

Feedback

Share one compliment you received today.

_____
_____
_____
_____

Awesome work!!

Gratitude

What are you thankful for today?

-
-
-
-

Affirmation

In truth, my gratitude is an absolute magnet for the manifestation of all that I want.

Achievements

What did you achieve today?
Big or small – they're all important.

-
-
-

Feedback

Share one compliment you received today.

Awesome work!!

Gratitude

What are you thankful for today?

-
-
-
-
-

Quote

"Thankfulness is the beginning of gratitude. Gratitude is the completion of thankfulness. Thankfulness may consist merely of words. Gratitude is shown in acts."
Henri Frederic Amiel

Achievements

What did you achieve today?
Big or small – they're all important.

-
-
-

Feedback

Share one compliment you received today.

Awesome work!!

Gratitude

What are you thankful for today?

- _____
  _____
  _____

- _____
  _____
  _____
  _____

- _____
  _____
  _____

- _____
  _____
  _____

- _____
  _____
  _____

Quote

"What separates privilege from entitlement is gratitude."
Brene Brown

Achievements

What did you achieve today?
Big or small – they're all important.

-
-
-

Feedback

Share one compliment you received today.

Awesome work!!

Gratitude

What are you thankful for today?

-
-
-
-
-

Affirmation

I feel gratitude for everything.

Achievements

What did you achieve today?
Big or small – they're all important.

-
-
-

Feedback

Share one compliment you received today.

Awesome work!!

Gratitude

What are you thankful for today?

-
-
-
-
-

Affirmation

I am learning to be grateful for what I have while being excited for what has yet to come.

Achievements

What did you achieve today?
Big or small – they're all important.

- _____
  _____
  _____

- _____
  _____
  _____

- _____
  _____
  _____

Feedback

Share one compliment you received today.

_____
_____
_____
_____

Awesome work!!

Gratitude

What are you thankful for today?

-
-
-
-
-

Quote

"When I started counting my blessings, my whole life turned around."
Willie Nelson

Achievements

What did you achieve today?
Big or small – they're all important.

- _____
  _____
  _____

- _____
  _____
  _____

- _____
  _____
  _____

Feedback

Share one compliment you received today.

_____
_____
_____
_____

Awesome work!!

Gratitude

What are you thankful for today?

- _____
  _____
  _____

- _____
  _____
  _____

- _____
  _____
  _____

- _____
  _____
  _____

- _____
  _____
  _____

Quote

"Gratitude is a currency that we can mint for ourselves and spend without fear of bankruptcy."
Fred De Witt Van Amburgh

Achievements

What did you achieve today?
Big or small – they're all important.

-
-
-

Feedback

Share one compliment you received today.

Awesome work!!

Gratitude

What are you thankful for today?

-
-
-
-
-

Affirmation

I am grateful now, and that is keeping the door open for more blessings.

Achievements

What did you achieve today?
Big or small – they're all important.

-
-
-

Feedback

Share one compliment you received today.

Awesome work!!

Gratitude

What are you thankful for today?

-

-

-

-

Affirmation

Whatever has happened, and whatever does happen, I'm certain that I can be grateful again.

Achievements

What did you achieve today?
Big or small – they're all important.

-
-
-

Feedback

Share one compliment you received today.

Awesome work!!

Gratitude

What are you thankful for today?

-
-
-
-
-

Quote

"Piglet noticed that even though he had a Very Small Heart, it could hold a rather large amount of Gratitude."
A.A. Milne

Achievements

What did you achieve today?
Big or small – they're all important.

-
-
-

Feedback

Share one compliment you received today.

Awesome work!!

Gratitude

What are you thankful for today?

- _____

- _____

- _____

- _____

- _____

Quote

"Forget yesterday it has already forgotten you. Don't sweat tomorrow you haven't even met. Instead, open your eyes and your heart to a truly precious gift today."
Steve Maraboli

Achievements

What did you achieve today?
Big or small – they're all important.

-
-
-

Feedback

Share one compliment you received today.

Awesome work!!

Gratitude

What are you thankful for today?

-
-
-
-

Affirmation

The feeling of gratefulness expands my perspective and opens me up to new ways of living happily in this world; it's as if the whole universe is in my heart.

Achievements

What did you achieve today?
Big or small – they're all important.

Feedback

Share one compliment you received today.

Awesome work!!

Gratitude

What are you thankful for today?

-
-
-
-
-

Affirmation

I give thanks for the helpful spirits and ancestors that guide me in this life journey.

Achievements

What did you achieve today?
Big or small – they're all important.

Feedback

Share one compliment you received today.

Awesome work!!

Gratitude

What are you thankful for today?

-
-
-
-
-

Quote

"The longer you linger in gratitude, the more you draw your new life to you. For gratitude is the ultimate state of receivership."
Dr. Joe Dispenza

Achievements

What did you achieve today?
Big or small – they're all important.

Feedback

Share one compliment you received today.

Awesome work!!

Gratitude

What are you thankful for today?

-
-
-
-
-

Quote

"Feeling gratitude and not expressing it is like wrapping a present and not giving it."
William Arthur Ward

Achievements

What did you achieve today?
Big or small – they're all important.

-
-
-

Feedback

Share one compliment you received today.

Awesome work!!

Gratitude

What are you thankful for today?

-
-
-
-
-

Quote

"Gratitude turns what we have into enough."
Anonymous.

Achievements

What did you achieve today?
Big or small – they're all important.

-
-
-

Feedback

Share one compliment you received today.

Awesome work!!

Gratitude

What are you thankful for today?

-
-
-
-
-

Quote

"The longer you linger in gratitude, the more you draw your new life to you. For gratitude is the ultimate state of receivership."
Dr. Joe Dispenza

Achievements

What did you achieve today?
Big or small – they're all important.

- _____

- _____

- _____

Feedback

Share one compliment you received today.

_____
_____
_____

Awesome work!!

Gratitude

What are you thankful for today?

-
-
-
-
-

Proverb

"'Enough' is a feast."
Buddhist proverb

Achievements

What did you achieve today?
Big or small – they're all important.

-
-
-

Feedback

Share one compliment you received today.

Awesome work!!

Gratitude

What are you thankful for today?

-
-
-
-
-

Quote

"Feeling gratitude and not expressing it is like wrapping a present and not giving it."
William Arthur Ward

Achievements

What did you achieve today?
Big or small – they're all important.

-
-
-

Feedback

Share one compliment you received today.

Awesome work!!

CONGRATULATIONS
ON REACHING DAY
60!!

Gratitude

Review your last 30 days of Gratitude and record your Top 5 here.

-
-
-
-
-

Achievements

Review your last 60 days of Achievements and record your Top 3.

- _____
  _____
  _____

- _____
  _____
  _____

- _____
  _____
  _____

Feedback

Review your last 60 days of Feedback and record your Top 2.

_____
_____
_____

YOU'RE TWO THIRDS OF THE WAY THERE!

Gratitude

What are you thankful for today?

-
-
-
-
-

Affirmation

I am grateful for excellent health, prosperity and true love.

Achievements

What did you achieve today?
Big or small – they're all important.

-

-

-

Feedback

Share one compliment you received today.

Awesome work!!

Gratitude

What are you thankful for today?

-
-
-
-
-

Affirmation

I am blessed.

Achievements

What did you achieve today?
Big or small – they're all important.

Feedback

Share one compliment you received today.

Awesome work!!

Gratitude

What are you thankful for today?

-
-
-
-
-

Quote

*"This a wonderful day.
I've never seen this one before."*
Maya Angelou

Achievements

What did you achieve today?
Big or small – they're all important.

- _____
- _____
- _____

Feedback

Share one compliment you received today.

_____

Awesome work!!

Gratitude

What are you thankful for today?

-
-
-
-
-

Quote

"Gratitude is not only the greatest of virtues, but the parent of all the others."
Cicero

Achievements

What did you achieve today?
Big or small – they're all important.

Feedback

Share one compliment you received today.

Awesome work!!

Gratitude

What are you thankful for today?

-
-
-
-
-

Quote

"Gratitude is riches. Complaint is poverty."
Doris Day

Achievements

What did you achieve today?
Big or small – they're all important.

-
-
-

Feedback

Share one compliment you received today.

Awesome work!!

Gratitude

What are you thankful for today?

-
-
-
-
-

Affirmation

I am so grateful for supportive friends and a loving family.

Achievements

What did you achieve today?
Big or small – they're all important.

-
-
-

Feedback

Share one compliment you received today.

Awesome work!!

Gratitude

What are you thankful for today?

-
-
-
-
-

Affirmation

All challenges are an opportunity for growth and I am thankful for the chance to evolve.

Achievements

What did you achieve today?
Big or small – they're all important.

-
-
-

Feedback

Share one compliment you received today.

Awesome work!!

Gratitude

What are you thankful for today?

-
-
-
-
-

Quote

"Some people grumble that roses have thorns; I am grateful that thorns have roses."
Alphonse Karr

Achievements

What did you achieve today?
Big or small – they're all important.

-
-
-

Feedback

Share one compliment you received today.

Awesome work!!

Gratitude

What are you thankful for today?

-
-
-
-
-

Quote

"Gratitude is the healthiest of all human emotions. The more you express gratitude for what you have, the more likely you will have even more to express gratitude for."
Zig Ziglar

Achievements

What did you achieve today?
Big or small – they're all important.

Feedback

Share one compliment you received today.

Awesome work!!

Gratitude

What are you thankful for today?

- _____
  _____
  _____
  _____

- _____
  _____
  _____
  _____

- _____
  _____
  _____
  _____

- _____
  _____
  _____
  _____

Affirmation

I am grateful for excellent health, prosperity and true love.

Achievements

What did you achieve today?
Big or small – they're all important.

-
-
-

Feedback

Share one compliment you received today.

Awesome work!!

Gratitude

What are you thankful for today?

-
-
-
-
-

Affirmation

In truth, my gratitude is an absolute magnet for the manifestation of all that I want.

Achievements

What did you achieve today?
Big or small – they're all important.

Feedback

Share one compliment you received today.

Awesome work!!

Gratitude

What are you thankful for today?

-
-
-
-
-

Quote

"Thankfulness is the beginning of gratitude. Gratitude is the completion of thankfulness. Thankfulness may consist merely of words. Gratitude is shown in acts."
Henri Frederic Amiel

Achievements

What did you achieve today?
Big or small – they're all important.

Feedback

Share one compliment you received today.

Awesome work!!

Gratitude

What are you thankful for today?

-
-
-
-
-

Quote

"What separates privilege from entitlement is gratitude."
Brene Brown

Achievements

What did you achieve today?
Big or small – they're all important.

-
-
-

Feedback

Share one compliment you received today.

Awesome work!!

Gratitude

What are you thankful for today?

-
-
-
-
-

Affirmation

I feel gratitude for everything.

Achievements

What did you achieve today?
Big or small – they're all important.

- _____
  _____
  _____

- _____
  _____
  _____

- _____
  _____
  _____

Feedback

Share one compliment you received today.

_____
_____
_____

Awesome work!!

Gratitude

What are you thankful for today?

-
-
-
-
-

Affirmation

I am learning to be grateful for what I have while being excited for what has yet to come.

Achievements

What did you achieve today?
Big or small – they're all important.

-
-
-

Feedback

Share one compliment you received today.

Awesome work!!

Gratitude

What are you thankful for today?

-
-
-
-
-

Quote

"When I started counting my blessings, my whole life turned around."
Willie Nelson

Achievements

What did you achieve today?
Big or small – they're all important.

-
-
-

Feedback

Share one compliment you received today.

Awesome work!!

Gratitude

What are you thankful for today?

- _____

- _____

- _____

- _____

Quote

"Gratitude is a currency that we can mint for ourselves and spend without fear of bankruptcy."
Fred De Witt Van Amburgh

Achievements

What did you achieve today?
Big or small – they're all important.

-
-
-

Feedback

Share one compliment you received today.

Awesome work!!

Gratitude

What are you thankful for today?

-
-
-
-
-

Affirmation

I am grateful now, and that is keeping the door open for more blessings.

Achievements

What did you achieve today?
Big or small – they're all important.

-
-
-

Feedback

Share one compliment you received today.

Awesome work!!

Gratitude

What are you thankful for today?

- _____
  _____
  _____
  _____

- _____
  _____
  _____
  _____

- _____
  _____
  _____
  _____

- _____
  _____
  _____
  _____

- _____
  _____
  _____
  _____

Affirmation

Whatever has happened, and whatever does happen, I'm certain that I can be grateful again.

Achievements

What did you achieve today?
Big or small – they're all important.

-
-
-

Feedback

Share one compliment you received today.

Awesome work!!

Gratitude

What are you thankful for today?

-
-
-
-
-

Quote

"Piglet noticed that even though he had a Very Small Heart, it could hold a rather large amount of Gratitude."
A.A. Milne

Achievements

What did you achieve today?
Big or small – they're all important.

-
-
-

Feedback

Share one compliment you received today.

Awesome work!!

Gratitude

What are you thankful for today?

-
-
-
-
-

Quote

"Forget yesterday it has already forgotten you. Don't sweat tomorrow you haven't even met. Instead, open your eyes and your heart to a truly precious gift today."
Steve Maraboli

Achievements

What did you achieve today?
Big or small – they're all important.

-
-
-

Feedback

Share one compliment you received today.

Awesome work!!

Gratitude

What are you thankful for today?

-
-
-
-
-

Quote

The feeling of gratefulness expands my perspective and opens me up to new ways of living happily in this world; it's as if the whole universe is in my heart.

Achievements

What did you achieve today?
Big or small – they're all important.

-
-
-

Feedback

Share one compliment you received today.

Awesome work!!

Gratitude

What are you thankful for today?

-
-
-
-

Affirmation

I give thanks for the helpful spirits and ancestors that guide me in this life journey.

Achievements

What did you achieve today?
Big or small – they're all important.

-
-
-

Feedback

Share one compliment you received today.

Awesome work!!

Gratitude

What are you thankful for today?

-
-
-
-
-

Quote

"The longer you linger in gratitude, the more you draw your new life to you. For gratitude is the ultimate state of receivership."
Dr. Joe Dispenza

Achievements

What did you achieve today?
Big or small – they're all important.

Feedback

Share one compliment you received today.

Awesome work!!

Gratitude

What are you thankful for today?

-
-
-
-

Quote

"Gratitude turns what we have into enough."
Anonymous

Achievements

What did you achieve today?
Big or small – they're all important.

-
-
-

Feedback

Share one compliment you received today.

Awesome work!!

Gratitude

What are you thankful for today?

-
-
-
-

Quote

"Gratitude is when memory is stored in the heart and not in the mind."
Lionel Hampton

Achievements

What did you achieve today?
Big or small – they're all important.

-
-
-

Feedback

Share one compliment you received today.

Awesome work!!

Gratitude

What are you thankful for today?

- _____
  _____
  _____

- _____
  _____
  _____

- _____
  _____
  _____

- _____
  _____
  _____

- _____
  _____
  _____

Quote

"Gratitude will shift you to a higher frequency, and you will attract much better things."
Rhonda Byrne

Achievements

What did you achieve today?
Big or small – they're all important.

-
-
-

Feedback

Share one compliment you received today.

Awesome work!!

Gratitude

What are you thankful for today?

-
-
-
-
-

Quote

"Gratitude makes sense of our past, brings peace for today, and creates a vision for tomorrow."
Melody Beattie

Achievements

What did you achieve today?
Big or small – they're all important.

- _____
  _____
  _____

- _____
  _____
  _____

- _____
  _____
  _____

Feedback

Share one compliment you received today.

_____
_____
_____
_____

Awesome work!!

Gratitude

What are you thankful for today?

-
-
-
-
-

Quote

"The more grateful I am, the more beauty I see."
Mary Davis

Achievements

What did you achieve today?
Big or small – they're all important.

-
-
-

Feedback

Share one compliment you received today.

Awesome work!!

CONGRATULATIONS
ON REACHING DAY
90!!

Gratitude

Review your last 30 days of Gratitude and record your Top 5 here.

-
-
-
-
-

Achievements

Review your last 90 days of Achievements and record your Top 3.

- _____
  _____
  _____

- _____
  _____
  _____

- _____
  _____
  _____

Feedback

Review your last 90 days of Feedback and record your Top 2.

_____
_____
_____

YOU HAVE NOW MADE THIS A LIFESTYLE.

Now What?

Congrats on reaching 90 days!!
You have now turned this task into a lifestyle.
To continue with this lifestyle – order a new journal at

www.thephoenixwithin.com.au/journal

Don't forget to tag us on social media and use

#todayiamgrateful
#thephoenixwithin

About the Author

Kylie King is a Multi-Award-Winning
Confidence and Business Coach, international speaker,
#1 Best selling author and founder of The Phoenix Within.

She is a MBA graduate who has studied NLP,
Time Line Therapy ® and Hypnotherapy.
She has years of experience in senior retail management
and leadership development.

Kylie works with the ladies who are ready to reclaim their power.
She supports and empowers you to uncover the tools
you already have within you, and allow your true uniqueness
to shine through, so you can confidently
move forward with power, passion and purpose.

She is a mum to two gorgeous girls and partner to Kim
and resides in the Blue Mountains, NSW, Australia.

Want to work with Kylie?

One-on-One Coaching and Mentoring

If you know it's time to make some changes in your life so that your business can thrive, get ready to be open and honest with where you're at and where you want to go.

With Kylie as your coach and your business cheerleader, you will be able to set some very specific and measurable goals and access the support and expertise needed to reach these milestones.

Through regular meetings with Kylie, you will work together to create structures and systems that will strengthen your business in both the short and long term and give you the forward momentum you need.

What's more, working with Kylie will give you the confidence and the growth mindset that are essential to the success of your business and personal life.

Invest in yourself today and contact Kylie

Email: kylie@thephoenixwithin.com.au

Facebook: www.Facebook.com/kyliekingphoenix

Instagram: @kyliekingphoenix

www.thephoenixwithin.com.au

Hypnotherapy

Kylie is also a Therapeutic Hypnotherapist.

Hypnotherapy is a fantastic tool and can help people improve their confidence and self-esteem.

Your unconscious mind aka inner voice can feel like your biggest critic causing you to feel bad about yourself, your actions and your thoughts. By accessing this during a session, your Hypnotherapist can help you to start to take control over these thoughts and how you feel about yourself.

Kylie holds Hypnotherapy sessions online via Zoom and Facebook or if you are local to Penrith or the Blue Mountains, face to face sessions can be arranged. Sessions are available 1 to 1 or also in a group setting.

Sessions can be tailored to your needs whether you need to boost your confidence, creativity or decrease procrastination.

Kylie also offer sessions so you can Quit Smoking, Loss Weight, Anxiety and delve into your Past Lives.

You can find out more here.
www.thephoenixwithin.com.au/services

Imposter Syndrome Quiz

Do you secretly worry that other people will find out that you are not as smart or capable at what you do as you think you are?

When you accomplish something, do you think "Phew, I fooled them this time, but I may not be so lucky next time?"

Do you live in fear of being found out, discovered, or unmasked?

If you answered "YES" to any of these questions, then you have encountered Imposter Syndrome. That feeling that you are just one step away from being found out as a complete fraud!

When we look at dealing with "Imposter Syndrome" it seems like such a big mountain to overcome. I was once told a quote, "How do you eat an elephant? One piece at a time."

To overcome this, I have broken down Imposter Syndrome as a whole, into five categories. This makes it easier to identify which one we are encountering so we know exactly the right course of action to take to keep it at bay.

The 5 categories or as I like to call them 'disguises' of Imposter Syndrome are:
1. The Perfectionist
2. The Superhero
3. The Natural Genius
4. The Soloist
5. The Expert

To find out which Imposter you are encountering, please take part in my free quiz which is available on my website – www.thephoenixwithin.com.au

The Little Book of Imposters

A pocket-sized guidebook to keep close at hand so you can overcome any Imposter that is dropping by for a visit.

This book outlines Imposter Syndrome. It breaks it down to the 5 different disguises and provides tips on how to overcome each one so you can continue your journey with clarity and focus.

Grab your copy here:
www.thephoenixwithin.com.au/imposterbook/

Notes

www.ingramcontent.com/pod-product-compliance
Lightning Source LLC
Chambersburg PA
CBHW072128160426
43197CB00012B/2033